WANKIE BIRDS

A guide to the common
birds of
Wankie National Park

Peter Steyn

LONGMAN RHODESIA

Longman Rhodesia (Pvt) Ltd
Beatrice Road, Southerton, Salisbury

*Associated companies, branches and
representatives throughout the world*

First published 1974

ISBN 0 582 64152 7

Printed in Rhodesia by Mardon Printers (Pvt) Limited, Salisbury

Contents

	page
Foreword	iv
Acknowledgements	v
Introduction	I
Silhouettes of some Wankie birds	4
Habitats	6
Species accounts	IO
A check list of birds recorded in Wankie National Park	49
Route list	55

Foreword

The Wankie National Park is the largest of Rhodesia's many parks and sanctuaries. It has acquired international recognition on account of its magnificent large mammal populations which, for variety at least, surpass those of most other sanctuaries in Africa. Nevertheless, Wankie is more than just a paradise of large mammals, and any discerning visitor will soon appreciate the complexity of its dynamic ecosystems of which the mammals are but one significant component. Another important element is provided by the outstanding birdlife comprising over four hundred different species.

An unfortunate tendency to overlook this fascinating segment of the fauna, unless it is drawn specifically to one's attention, leads to many park visitors unwittingly denying themselves the pleasures to be derived from quietly watching birds going about their daily lives. It is a relaxing pursuit that can be followed at almost any time in any part of the park, and the satisfaction it yields to the unobtrusive observer is often highlighted by the confidence transmitted to other animals by undisturbed birds. Many species react to each other and large mammals are often alerted to potential danger by the way in which birds behave, so that by sitting quietly and allowing birds to act normally one often enhances one's chances of witnessing something 'special'.

This book, written by a very competent author and photographer, will fulfil the long felt need to focus more attention on the birdlife in the park. It provides a handy source of reference which will be useful and informative to a wide audience, ranging from the most casual birdwatcher to the serious student of ornithology. For the former, there is a ready means of identifying eighty of the most conspicuous species to be found in the park as well as some information on their biology, while for the latter there is an up-to-date check list of all the species so far recorded in Wankie.

I have no hesitation in commending this book to our many visitors to Wankie; I am sure it will do much to enhance their appreciation of this magnificent park through a better understanding of the birds that occur there and which are such an important part of our natural heritage.

Graham Child
DIRECTOR
NATIONAL PARKS AND WILD LIFE MANAGEMENT

Acknowledgements

The Department of National Parks and Wild Life Management gave me enthusiastic support in the preparation of this book, and I am grateful to the Director, Dr Graham Child, for his encouragement and for generously contributing a Foreword.

Mr Boyd Reese, Regional Warden, and the Wardens of Main, Sinamatella and Robins camps, Messrs Derek Williams, Harry Cantel and Cliff Freeman respectively, gave me generous assistance in many ways. The help of the following members of the National Parks staff is also gratefully acknowledged: Messrs Kerry Fynn, John Herbert, Bill Howells, Norman Payne, Bob Reyers, John Rushworth, John Stevens, Carl Vernon and Basil Williamson.

Mention should be made of Mr Ted Davison's pioneer list of three hundred and forty-six species which was published in *The South African Avifauna Series* (No. 13) in 1963. This proved a valuable source of reference.

The preparation of the check list for this book was undertaken in co-operation with Mr Bill Howells, and we should like to acknowledge records supplied by Dr and Mrs Alan Kemp, Mr Carl Vernon and Mrs Pat Lorber, all of whom added new species for the park.

I should particularly like to thank Mr John Rushworth for his help in the preparation of the simplified vegetation map of the park.

It did not prove possible to photograph all the birds for the book myself, but the few remaining gaps were filled by fellow bird-photographers who generously donated their pictures. The following are details of photographs supplied:

Mr Dave Barbour	:	Arnot's Chat (plate 20)
Mr Cyril Laubscher	:	White Helmet Shrike (plate 16)
		Yellow-eye Canary (plate 20)
Mr Nico Myburgh	:	Pied Babbler (plate 20)
Mr Ken Newman	:	Grey Hornbill (plate 12)
		Red-winged Starling (plate 16)

Mr Graeme Arnott drew the page of silhouettes and the vegetation map, and I am indebted to him for the many hours he devoted to this work.

Finally, my thanks are due to my wife, Jenny, who patiently unravelled my execrable handwriting and typed the text of this book.

Introduction

Wankie National Park is a spectacular game reserve that ranks second only to the Victoria Falls as Rhodesia's major tourist attraction. During the dry season visitors can watch a herd of some sixty elephants drinking at a water-hole, while in the background graceful giraffes splay out their front legs in the apparently complicated process of getting their heads down to water level. Although such sights are fascinating, there eventually comes a limit to the number of litres one can watch an elephant squirt down its throat. It is then that the more perceptive observer notices the black and white plover at the elephant's feet, or the garrulous brown birds clambering on a giraffe's neck, and wonders what they are. The purpose of this book is to help him identify them.

When this book was written, four hundred and one species of birds had been identified in Wankie National Park. When one realizes that this is two-thirds of the total number of birds recorded in Rhodesia, then the richness of the avifauna of the park may be appreciated. But it is this very wealth of birdlife that posed an immediate problem when preparing this guide: just which species should be included and which left out?

The sub-title would have been cumbersome, but more accurate, had it read 'A guide to the common *and conspicuous* birds of Wankie National Park', for however common a species may be, it would need to catch the attention of the average visitor to merit inclusion. Thus there is an immediate bias towards the choice of large, striking or colourful birds at the expense of what bird-watchers call L.B.J.s or 'Little Brown Jobs'. This method of selection is best illustrated by the fact that five of the seven hornbills that occur (two are rare in the park) are dealt with, while no larks, warblers or nocturnal species are included. This bias is undoubtedly realistic, especially as one cannot leave one's vehicle for a closer look at an elusive 'Little Brown Job'.

Using the above criteria, eighty species, or somewhat less than a quarter

I

of the park's total, have been selected for inclusion. This number may be considered too limited by some, but it must be remembered that this guide is designed for those with little knowledge of birds and for tourists from overseas to whom everything is new.

The page of silhouettes is designed as an introduction to some of the species which have a characteristic shape, but it is not intended to be comprehensive and the scale is approximate. In view of the varying photographic conditions and lenses used, on no account should the colour plates be used as an indication of a bird's size. Incidentally, many of the photographs illustrating this book were taken in the park from a car window using a 500 mm lens resting on a sandbag. The possibilities for bird-photography are unlimited, and the photographer's chances are enhanced by the tameness of many birds in the camps and picnic sites.

Some explanation of the seasons is necessary for the visitor to Rhodesia, particularly if he comes from a temperate environment where the four seasons are clearly defined. It is logical to start with 'the rains', which cover our summer, commencing at the end of October and lasting into March. Thereafter there is a gradual merging into the dry season or winter, the coldest months of which are June, July and August. Although daytime temperatures may be hot, they are not uncomfortably so, and the nights can be very cold indeed. During September the weather warms up progressively, until the climax of heat is reached in October, often referred to as 'suicide month' in Rhodesia. This period may be loosely termed 'spring' as the leafless trees bud with new foliage before the rains come. Finally, the heavens darken, and the year turns full circle with the advent of the first cataclysmic storm that releases the parched earth from its dusty bondage.

Linked to the seasons is an important change in the bird population. During the period from September to March, there is an influx of migrants to Rhodesia. These fall into two categories: the long distance or palaearctic migrants from Europe and Asia, and the intra-African migrants that come from further north in Africa. Both groups have in common the fact that they have the best of both worlds as far as food supply is concerned. Amongst the palaearctic migrants are such species as the White Stork, Wood Sandpiper and European Bee-eater, while the intra-African migrants include the Woolly-necked Stork, White-bellied Stork, Yellow-billed Kite, Carmine Bee-eater and Paradise Flycatcher. While it may be felt that the absence of these species in the dry season should disqualify them from inclusion, they are only a small proportion of the total and are very characteristic of the Wankie scene during the rains. Indeed, the rainy season is the best time to visit the park for birds, and the presence of these interesting migrant species fully compensates for the closure of the Robins area at this time. Also, it is during this period that the herds of game disperse widely, and the visitor is able to make up for the lack of big game viewing by identifying the birds.

Place names used in the text may all be found on the tourist map that is automatically given out to visitors at their first point of entry into the park.

The standard bird book in use in southern Africa is *Roberts Birds of South Africa* (1970 edition), and the names used in this guide have been taken from *Roberts*, as it is generally called. Each species dealt with is given a *Roberts* number to facilitate cross-referencing.

For the more advanced bird-watcher, a check list of the birds recorded in Wankie National Park is given at the back of the book. The list of four hundred and one birds will not remain the final total, for there are some forty species which are likely to occur that remain unrecorded so far. The challenge is there for the more experienced bird-watcher, and some exciting finds are possible. Just such a case was the discovery of a single Golden Pipit at Main Camp in 1972. It proved to be the second record for southern Africa, the previous one being from the Transvaal in 1906.

Also at the back of the book will be found a list of the eighty species dealt with in the main text. This has been designed so that birds seen on a particular route can be recorded, and it is hoped that this will increase the visitor's interest and enjoyment during his time in the park.

Finally, although this book has been compiled specifically for Wankie National Park, it is by no means limited to the park. It may be used to a certain extent throughout Rhodesia, but particularly in the drier western areas.

Silhouettes
of some Wankie birds
(to approximate scale only)

1	White-backed Vulture	24	Hamerkop
2	Bateleur	25	Crowned Plover
3	Yellow-billed Kite	26	Red-crested Korhaan
4	White-backed Vulture	27	Capped Wheatear
5	Yellow-billed Kite	28	Hoopoe
6	European Bee-eater	29	Namaqua Dove
7	Lilac-breasted Roller	30	Crested Barbet
8	Red-billed Hoopoe	31	Yellow-billed Hornbill
9	Paradise Flycatcher	32	Double-banded Sandgrouse
10	Fish Eagle	33	Turtle Dove
11	Masked Weaver	34	Coqui Francolin
12	White-browed Sparrow-weaver	35	Swainson's Francolin
13	Grey Loerie	36	Knob-billed Duck
14	Scarlet-chested Sunbird	37	Red-billed Teal
15	Pied Kingfisher	38	Grey Heron
16	Black-eyed Bulbul	39	Secretary Bird
17	Tawny Eagle	40	White-bellied Stork
18	Long-tailed Starling	41	Crowned Guineafowl
19	Blue-eared Glossy Starling	42	Yellow-billed Oxpeckers
20	Meyer's Parrot	43	Saddlebill
21	Pied Babbler	44	Marabou
22	Long-tailed Shrike	45	Crowned Crane
23	Fork-tailed Drongo	46	Ground Hornbill

G G Arnott

5

Habitats

The vegetation map (figure 1) indicates the main habitats of the park, but it is much simplified so as not to confuse the visitor unnecessarily. Basically, bearing in mind that the mixed scrub woodland is on Kalahari sand too, there are two broad divisions into the vegetation found on the Kalahari sand that extends from Main Camp as far as Shumba, and the mopane woodland occurring west of Shumba, which is the point of transition between the two. But this is very much a generalization, and there are a number of habitats within these two main ones.

Perhaps the best way of introducing the visitor to the habitats he encounters is to travel with him through the park on the main route from Main Camp to Robins via Sinamatella. Should he enter at the Robins end, he will then pass through these habitats in reverse order. Naturally there will be variations when he travels by subsidiary routes, but he should have no difficulty in recognizing the main habitat types.

Between the entrance gate and Main Camp we pass through teak woodland in which the Rhodesian teak tree, *Baikiaea plurijuga*, is the dominant species; it gives the name *Baikiaea* to this type of woodland. Although thinned out, there are still many teak trees in Main Camp itself (figure 2). Main Camp is also on the edge of an area of thorn trees, or acacia woodland, which is well developed in places to the south of Main Camp on the direct road to Ngweshla Pan (figure 3). Consequently it is rich in birdlife, and in a stroll of half an hour round the camp a competent bird-watcher should easily identify thirty species. The beginner should see at least a dozen or so of the birds dealt with in this book, including Laughing Dove, Bradfield's Hornbill, Fork-tailed Drongo, Arrow-marked Babbler, Pied Babbler, Black-eyed Bulbul, Kurrichane Thrush, Groundscraper Thrush, Paradise Flycatcher (in summer), Long-tailed Shrike, Blue-eared Glossy Starling, White-browed Sparrow-weaver, House Sparrow, Grey-headed Sparrow and Masked Weaver. If he is lucky, he may also see the beautiful Crimson-breasted Shrike in the thorn trees along the western fence of the camp.

The bird-watching potential in the camps and picnic sites is one of the most enjoyable features of the park. Not only is there a chance to stretch one's legs, but the birds are usually very tame. Also, these places always have a bird-bath, and by sitting quietly near one it is possible to see a cross-section of the birds occurring in the area.

On driving out of Main Camp, we are immediately in very open country with scattered thorn trees. Within a short while species likely to be seen are Red-billed Francolin, Swainson's Francolin, Crowned Guineafowl, Crowned Plover, Grey Loerie, Lilac-breasted Roller, Ground Hornbill and White-crowned Shrike. In the rains this list would probably be augmented by Woolly-necked Stork, White Stork, Knob-billed Duck, Yellow-billed Kite, European Bee-eater and Carmine Bee-eater.

Assuming that we are heading directly to Nyamandhlovu Pan, we will drive through mixed scrub woodland from Dom Pan onwards. This is a rather nondescript type of 'bushveld' with vegetation that is usually two to three metres in height (figure 4). Most of the birds seen in this environment are likely to be seen in other habitats too, but two birds to be particularly watched for are the Coqui Francolin and Red-crested Korhaan.

The viewing platform at Nyamandhlovu Pan is an excellent spot for bird-watching, despite the bare appearance of the area round the pan itself (figure 5). As it is filled artificially, the pan is full all year round, and thus provides a stable habitat. If they have not already been seen, the Yellow-billed Hornbill and Blue-eared Glossy Starling will almost certainly be met with here. One of the most characteristic species is the Blacksmith Plover, which is often to be seen feeding amongst elephant droppings. A careful scrutiny of the water's edge through binoculars (which are recommended) will usually reveal a Three-banded Sandplover. During the summer months the Wood Sandpiper will be spotted too, and away from the water may be seen groups of White-bellied Storks which like to forage in open areas. At various times of the day Turtle Doves will fly in to drink. The arid environment is also to the liking of the Capped Wheatear, which should be watched for in the dry season. From one's elevated position on the viewing platform it is often possible to see Ostriches feeding in the distance.

Travelling on towards Shumba, the bushveld habitat tends to become rather monotonous, particularly in the dry season, but it is always worth turning off to each pan along the way, and Guvalala Pan should certainly

7

not be missed. In the dry season there is a remarkable concentration of Crowned Plovers between Danga Pan and Shumba, with pairs often only a few hundred metres apart. If a careful watch is kept, the plovers may be seen sitting on their nests situated on the road verges. These verges are artificially cleared (figure 4) and the resultant open swath attracts many species which are able to see insects in this cleared area more easily. One should not omit to mention that it would be unusual not to find at least some of the vultures and birds of prey mentioned in the text, and the Bateleur is most likely to be seen as it sweeps rapidly through the sky.

At last Shumba picnic site is reached, and it is the most attractive stopping place in the park. In its centre is a magnificent fig tree which casts its shade over the whole area. Here, probably for the first time, will be seen the Long-tailed Starling, and from now on it is common. Another species resident here is the Red-winged Starling, and Shumba is one of the few places where it may be seen.

Westwards of Shumba the country undergoes a dramatic change, and the sand gives way to the dark soil on which grows the dominant mopane woodland (figure 6). In the dry season, when it is leafless, it gives the impression of being stark and lifeless, but the fallen leaves provide valuable nutrition for the animals. When one least expects it, a flash of black and white draws one's attention to an Arnot's Chat, a small dapper species that is typical of mopane woodland. Other species likely to be seen are Double-banded Sandgrouse, Red-billed Hoopoe, Red-billed Hornbill and White Helmet Shrike.

Now for the first time we notice hills and granite outcrops, for one of the features of the Kalahari sand environment is its flatness. Sinamatella is perched on a high hill, but mopane woodland remains the dominant habitat. Here Red-winged Starlings may be seen again, as well as many Long-tailed Starlings, and the Boubou which is a common camp bird. Near the office is an attractive aloe garden, and when these are in flower the Scarlet-chested Sunbird should be watched for.

Between Sinamatella and Robins there are large dams such as Mandavu and Deteema (figure 7), and here species to watch for include the Grey Heron, Great White Egret, Hamerkop, Saddlebill, Egyptian Goose, Fish Eagle and Pied Kingfisher.

As we approach Robins the country becomes progressively more open, and there are large areas of grassland. Although mopane woodland is still dominant, it is now mixed with areas of terminalia woodland, the main tree species of which is the Mangwe *Terminalia sericea*. Here also are marshy open areas or vleis, usually artificially filled, and a good example is Little Toms where there is an observation hut. If they have not been seen before, then species such as the Blue Waxbill, Yellow-eye Canary and Golden-breasted Bunting are likely to be seen as they come to drink in such a spot.

Robins Camp terminates our journey through the park, and a species to look for here is Meyer's Parrot. Needless to say, the White-browed Sparrow-weaver is present in force, and it must surely merit first place as the most characteristic and widespread species in the park.

Species accounts

1 OSTRICH (R.1)
Plate 1

Identification The Ostrich is the largest living bird. The males are a little over two metres in height and may weigh as much as one hundred and fifty kilograms. This species can not be mistaken for any other. The males have black plumage while that of the females and immatures of both sexes is a dull grey-brown. Newly hatched chicks, if one is lucky enough to see them, are delightful creatures. They have coarse straw coloured down that sticks up and gives them a hedgehog-like appearance, and on the head and neck they have longitudinal streaking which serves as an effective camouflage.

Distribution This species may be encountered throughout the park, but it avoids thick woodland and is generally to be found in drier more open areas. It is likely to be seen in the Robins area.

Notes The Ostrich is primarily a vegetarian, but it also swallows pebbles to help grind up its food. Small groups made up of a male and a few females and sub-adults are normally seen. During courtship the male waves his wings about, thus displaying the white plumes at the ends like flags; these were the feathers most sought after by the millinery trade when they were the fashion. The nest is merely a scrape in the ground in which the pitted creamy eggs are laid. Although they have a capacity of about twenty-four hen's eggs, they are nevertheless only 1,4 % of the female's body weight and are small for the size of the bird. The clutch varies from about ten to twenty-five eggs, and even more have been found; these larger clutches are generally the work of two or more females. The incubation period lasts about forty days and the male does much of the incubation which includes the night

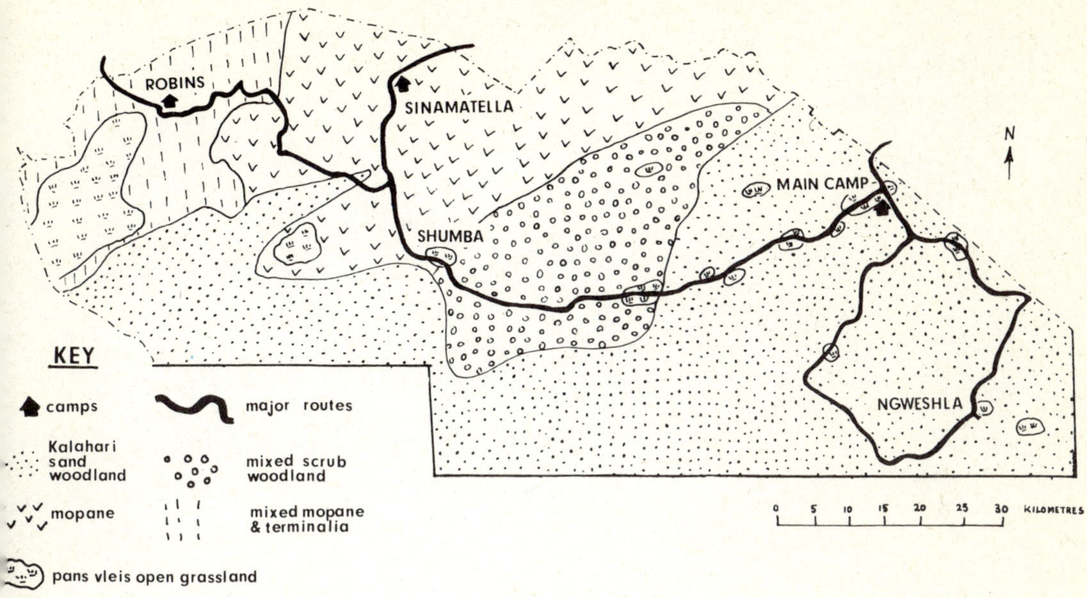

KEY

- camps
- Kalahari sand woodland
- mopane
- pans vleis open grassland

- major routes
- mixed scrub woodland
- mixed mopane & terminalia

ROBINS

SINAMATELLA

MAIN CAMP

SHUMBA

NGWESHLA

N

0 5 10 15 20 25 30 KILOMETRES

Fig. 1 Simplified vegetation map of Wankie National Park

Fig. 2 View of Main Camp showing Rhodesian teak trees
(January)

Fig. 3 Acacia thornveld on the road from Main Camp to Ngweshla Pan (October)

Fig. 4 Mixed scrub woodland near Nyamandhlovu Pan (January)

Fig. 5 View of Nyamandhlovu Pan (October)

Fig. 6 Mopane woodland (November)

Fig. 7 Mandavu Dam viewed from the wall

Fig. 8 The vlei at Little Toms (October)

shift. He is relieved by the female at various times during the day. Despite the number of eggs laid, very few chicks survive to maturity. They are preyed upon by a number of mammalian predators and larger birds of prey such as eagles.

2 GREY HERON (R.54)
Plate 2

Identification This graceful heron, which stands about a metre in height, may be identified by its grey colour, yellow bill, white front to the neck which has some black streaking, and by the black band that extends from above the eye to the back of the head.

Distribution This species is sparingly but widely distributed wherever there is water. During the rains it may move to areas that have become temporarily inundated.

Notes It is usually seen standing alone in shallow water where it remains immobile for long periods as it watches for its prey. This consists of frogs, fish and other aquatic life; occasionally mice and small birds are captured too in vegetation near the water's edge.

3 GREAT WHITE EGRET (R.58)
Plate 2

Identification The large size, long slender neck and pure white plumage distinguish this egret from the Cattle Egret (see next species). The bill may be either yellow or black.

Distribution Like the Grey Heron it is nowhere common, and it is always associated with water.

Notes It hunts in similar fashion to the Grey Heron and, although its diet is similar, it would tend to take smaller prey. Its habit of wading in water serves further to distinguish it from the Cattle Egret which rarely wades.

4 CATTLE EGRET (R.61)
Plate 3

Identification The popular name 'Tick-bird' is perhaps the most useful guide to the identification of this species. It associates regularly with cattle and big game, usually in flocks, and it was once believed that it fed mainly on ticks pecked off these animals. However, it is now generally accepted that it walks with grazing animals so as to catch the insects they disturb. The bill is always yellow and there are buff patches on top of the head, back and breast which assume a richer colour when it is in breeding condition.

Distribution It is found throughout the park in association with game, generally in open areas where the vegetation is not too rank.

Notes This species does not breed in the park and there are very few breeding sites known in Rhodesia. It nests colonially in large numbers, quite often in association with other species of egrets, herons and cormorants. After breeding young birds disperse widely, and one nestling ringed in South Africa was recovered three months later 2 700 kilometres to the north in the Congo.

5 HAMERKOP (R.72)
Plate 3

Identification Its name, derived from Afrikaans, means 'Hammerhead' and this gives the key to its identification. At the back of its head it has a large crest which, together with its large black bill, gives the impression of a hammer. Its colour is a uniform sepia brown and the legs are black. The call is a maniacal high-pitched trilling note.

Distribution It occurs throughout the park wherever there is water.

Notes This species feeds on aquatic life and hunts in shallow water; it has the habit of shuffling its feet in the mud as it progresses so as to disturb its food. For its size (it is only fifty-five centimetres in length) the Hamerkop builds a remarkably large nest. This is a hollow domed structure of sticks that weighs some ninety kilograms and would fit with difficulty on top of a wheelbarrow. An incredible assortment of rubbish is usually placed on top of the nest and such items as old bones, rags, rusty tins and tortoise shells have been recorded. Despite the size of the nest, the small entrance hole in one side is just large enough to admit the birds. Nests are placed in the fork of a tree or on a cliff ledge, and the entrance overhangs the drop so as to discourage predators. Amongst primitive Africans the Hamerkop is considered a portentous bird and it is much feared.

6 MARABOU (R.73)
Plate 1

Identification   This large stork is noted for its rather grotesque appearance, and its usual hunched stance with neck drawn in does nothing to lessen this impression. It has a large wedge-shaped bill, and the bare pink neck and head are covered by sparse white down. The underparts are white and the feathers of its back and wings are blue-grey. Although the legs are black, they are frequently covered with white matter; this is because the bird defecates on its own legs so as to cool itself. This interesting phenomenon is also found in other storks.

Distribution   This species may be seen throughout the park.

Notes   The Marabou is usually to be found feeding on carrion in association with vultures, but it eats insects and small vertebrates too. It is also an important predator of breeding Red-billed Queleas, which are pestilential grain eaters that nest in colonies of hundreds of thousands on occasions. At other times, particularly in drying pools, it feeds on frogs, fish and other aquatic life. The main known breeding area in southern Africa is in the Okavango swamps in Botswana.

7 SADDLEBILL (R.75)
Plate 1

Identification   This spectacular stork stands one and a half metres in height and is readily identified by its colourful appearance. The body is black and white, the neck black and the bill red with a broad band of black across the middle. It derives its name from the yellow 'saddle' at the junction of its bill and forehead. The 'knee' joints and feet are pink. In flight it shows a great deal of white in the wings. If a good view is obtained, males and females may be distinguished. The female has a yellow eye, while that of the male is dark brown; he also has two small yellow wattles beneath his chin. Young birds leave the nest in drab brown plumage.

Distribution   It is likely to be seen wherever there is water and in the rainy season may be found in shallow flooded areas.

Notes   The diet of this species is mainly aquatic life, but it will also feed on termites away from water when these are swarming. The Saddlebill breeds in the park and the large stick nest is placed on top of a tree. The eggs are laid about February.

8 WOOLLY-NECKED STORK (R.77)
Plate 2

Identification   The impression is of a glossy black stork with a white neck that has the appearance of being covered with cotton wool. The forehead is black, and the bill is dark with a reddish tip. The feathers of the upper breast are loose and appear shaggy. The abdomen is white.

Distribution   It is found in open areas during the rainy season, usually where there is shallow water.

Notes   This species is somewhat of a puzzle. It is known to breed solitarily at Chipinga in Rhodesia and in Zululand in South Africa. However, it seems mainly to be a migrant from areas to the north of Rhodesia which comes south during the rainy season. It is locally quite common, occuring in small flocks, and it may usually be seen round Main Camp in areas of open grassland.

9 WHITE-BELLIED STORK (R.78)
Plate 2

Identification This species may be recognized by the fact that it is mainly black in colour with a contrasting white abdomen. It has bare skin on its face which is red round the eye and blue below it. In flight it shows a white rump.

Distribution It is found throughout the park in open areas.

Notes One of the best guides to the identification of this species is that it occurs in large flocks during the rainy season. It is a migrant from Africa north of the equator where it breeds. It feeds on insects such as locusts, army worms and termites and does much good in helping to control local outbreaks.

10 WHITE STORK (R.80)
Plate 1

Identification It may be readily identified by its white body which contrasts with its black wing tips. The bill and legs are red.

Distribution This is a bird of open areas and it is found throughout the park. It is fond of shallow flooded areas such as occur round Main Camp during the rains.

Notes Its diet is similar to that of the White-bellied Stork, but it also includes aquatic life such as frogs. It is a migrant from Europe and Asia where it breeds, occurring in Africa as far south as Cape Town during the northern winter. Although still seen in substantial flocks at times, this species is not as abundant as it was formerly. The reason for this is a serious decline in the European stork population caused by pollution and the disappearance of its habitat. During the last decade a small breeding population has become established in the south-west Cape Province of South Africa.

11 EGYPTIAN GOOSE (R.89)
Plate 4

Identification   The main colour of this species is brown, pale on the under-parts and dark on the back. There is a dark patch of brown round the yellow eye and also a small round patch in the centre of the breast. The latter feature gave it its Afrikaans name 'Kolgans' which means 'Target-goose'. In flight it reveals a large patch of white at the bend of the wing.

Distribution   It occurs on permanent water at dams such as Deteema and Mandavu, but during the rains it will move into flooded areas.

Notes   This goose is usually found in pairs grazing along the shore or resting on islands or banks. It lays its eggs in the disused nests of large birds such as eagles, or on top of a Hamerkop's nest. The goslings are able to fall a considerable distance to the ground without injuring themselves. It will also nest in rank vegetation on an island. Whatever the nest site, it is always thickly lined with the down of the incubating female.

12 KNOB-BILLED DUCK (R.91)
Plate 3

Identification   This duck may be identified by its dark green iridescent back and wings, which contrast with its white underparts. The neck is speckled in both sexes. The best single feature that aids identification is the fleshy knob on the bill of the male; it is largest in the breeding season during the rains.

Distribution   It may be found near water in all areas throughout the year, but it is commonest during the rains. At this time of year it may be quite often seen in the Main Camp area.

Notes   This species grazes on grass seeds, but it also feeds on aquatic insects. It frequently perches in trees, and the usual nest site is a hole in a tree. Ringing recoveries show that this duck may move considerable distances and birds ringed in Rhodesia have been recovered as far afield as Lake Chad and the Sudan.

13 RED-BILLED TEAL (R.97)
Plate 3

Identification This brown duck may be readily distinguished by its red bill, pale cheeks and dark brown top to its head. In flight it reveals a broad band of white on the hind edge of the wing.

Distribution It is found throughout the park in association with water.

Notes This is the duck most likely to be encountered on any permanent water throughout the year. It occurs in small flocks in the dry season, but during its breeding season in the rains it may be found in pairs on flooded pans. It makes a nest in vegetation near water.

14 SECRETARY BIRD (R.105)
Plate 4

Identification This species gives the impression of a long-legged terrestrial eagle. The red face, grey plumage, long tail and black feathers projecting at the back of the head make it easy to identify.

Distribution It is found throughout the park in open areas where the vegetation is fairly short.

Notes The name of this species is derived from the feathers at the back of its head which were likened to the quill pen placed behind the ear of a scribe. It walks with a measured stride over the veld and eats almost anything it can capture, from insects to young hares. It kills its prey by stamping on it, but when dealing with a snake the wings are spread out to draw its strikes until it is tired and can be safely killed. The nest is a platform of sticks placed on top of a thorn tree, usually at no great height. It is used outside the breeding season as a roost.

15 WHITE-BACKED VULTURE (R.107)
Plate 5

Identification This is the most common vulture found in the park and it may be identified by its mainly brown appearance. The head and neck are unfeathered except for a sparse covering of down. Adults usually reveal a white back when taking off, but this feature is not constant. Young birds are darker brown than adults and are streaky below. The silhouette page shows the characteristic flight outline of vultures.

Distribution It is found in all areas.

Notes Vultures soar at a great height where they may be only just visible to the human eye. They spread out over a vast area and as soon as one drops down to carrion all the others follow suit in a chain-reaction. Once they are at the carcass, the scene may be likened to an all-in wrestling match as birds bound in and push others aside to an accompaniment of squeals and hisses. They will often perch in trees in groups, usually after they have fed or while they wait for a predator such as a lion to leave the scene of a kill. Despite the distaste that most people have for them, they are in fact remarkably clean birds and bathe regularly. The stick nest is placed at the very top of a tall tree and receives no protection from the sun.

16 LAPPET-FACED VULTURE (R.108)
Plate 5

Identification This is the largest of the vultures, having an enormous wingspan of about three metres. Its most distinguishing feature is its reddish face. The bill is very large and powerful. At the base of the bare neck it has a ruff of feathers. The main colour is black, but it has white legs and underparts, the latter heavily streaked with dark feathers. In flight it appears to be an almost wholly black bird with white leggings.

Distribution It is found throughout the park.

Ostrich (male)   Marabou

PLATE 1

Saddlebill   White Stork

Woolly-necked Stork

Great White Egret

PLATE 2

White-bellied Stork

Grey Heron

Hamerkop

Cattle Egret

PLATE 3

Knob-billed Duck (male)

Red-billed Teal

Crowned Crane

Secretary Bird

PLATE 4

Red-crested Korhaan

Egyptian Goose

Notes This imposing vulture is usually found in small numbers at a carcass. It is often to be seen standing apart from the common throng, but when it decides to bound in to feed all the other vultures give way to it. It builds a huge nest of sticks on a very low flat-topped tree, in the manner of a Secretary Bird.

17 WHITE-HEADED VULTURE (R.109)
Plate 5

Identification This species is the most attractive of all the vultures. It derives its name from the white down on top of its head. Its bill is red at the tip and blue at the base. When perched, the dark colouration is relieved by white on its abdomen and wings. In flight it reveals conspicuous patches of white on the underwing.

Distribution It occurs throughout the park.

Notes Although it joins other vultures at carrion, it may often be encountered solitarily. It has been known to kill its own prey at times.

18 YELLOW-BILLED KITE (R.129)
Plate 6

Identification This brown hawk may be readily identified by its forked tail (see silhouettes) and yellow bill. It is very graceful on the wing and has the characteristic of twisting its tail in flight. Although occasional individuals may be seen throughout the year, the main bulk of the population moves to the north of Rhodesia in the dry season. During the rains it is common. However, it is frequently outnumbered at this time by the very similar Black Kite, which is a migrant from Europe and Asia and occurs in flocks of hundreds of birds. The Black Kite is distinguished from the Yellow-billed Kite by having a black tip to its bill and more white on top of its head.

Distribution It occurs throughout the park.

Notes This species preys on a wide variety of small mammals, birds and reptiles. It is very partial to termites, usually capturing and eating these in flight. It builds a nest of sticks which is lined with all manner of rubbish such as scraps of paper, dung, hair, wool and old rags. It was this partiality for bits and pieces that Shakespeare had noted when he wrote in *The Winter's Tale* 'when the kite builds, look to lesser linen'. He was referring to the Red Kite, once common in Britain, and even occurring in the streets of London, but now almost extinct there except for a few pairs in Wales.

19 BLACK-SHOULDERED KITE (R.130)
Plate 6

Identification This small hawk is grey above and white below. On its shoulders it has black patches from which it gets its name. When seen from below in flight it appears mostly white, but the tips of the wings are black. It has the habit of hovering in one spot on winnowing wings and this is a very useful guide to identification.

Distribution It is found throughout the park, but not in thick woodland. It prefers an open grassy habitat such as may be found in the Robins and Main Camp areas.

Notes This species preys mostly on mice, doing most of its hunting while hovering, but it also watches for its prey from a perch. It tends to move in and out of areas, probably taking advantage of local explosions in the rodent population. It constructs a small stick nest which is usually placed on top of a thorn tree.

20 TAWNY EAGLE (R.134)
Plate 6

Identification The plumage of this large eagle is rather variable, but most individuals are tawny with varying amounts of darker brown on the shoulders, back and the breast. Some birds in faded plumage appear almost white, and young birds in their first year out of the nest are pale reddish.

It has a fine head with a strongly hooked black bill which has a fleshy yellow covering to the upper mandible at its junction with the head. This is called the cere and it is a feature found in all birds of prey. The feathered leggings extend right down to the feet.

Distribution   It is found in all areas.

Notes   This is the commonest resident eagle in the park. Its diet is varied and it will feed on carrion or kill its own prey up to the size of a guineafowl or hare. At other times it is piratical and will rob other birds of their food. The nest is built on top of a flat-topped tree and two eggs are laid in May or June. During the rains a similar species called the Steppe Eagle migrates south from eastern Europe and Asia. This eagle may be distinguished from the Tawny Eagle by the fact that it occurs in large flocks and spends much of its time on the ground running after emerging termites, its principal food while in southern Africa.

21   FISH EAGLE   (R.149)
Plate 6

Identification   This striking eagle is easily identified by its white head, breast and back which are offset against its black wings and chestnut underparts. The bare skin of the face is yellow. In flight it appears dark except for its white head and tail. Young birds are brown with a white band across the chest and a dull whitish tail which has a dark terminal band. They gradually moult into adult plumage over a period of four to five years. The call is a ringing 'yeeee, kow, kow, kowkowkow' and is one of the most haunting and characteristic sounds of the wilder parts of Africa.

Distribution   It always occurs in association with water and should be watched for at dams such as Deteema and Mandavu.

Notes   This eagle is adapted for catching fish and has bare legs and rough pads on its feet. It hunts from a perch and drops down onto its prey in a long shallow dive. Sometimes, if it catches a fish too heavy to lift, it will paddle to the shore using its wings. In addition to fish, it also preys on other waterbirds, young crocodiles and small mammals. It builds a large nest of sticks in a tree near water and lays its eggs about June.

22 BATELEUR (R.151)
Plate 5

Identification This imposing eagle has the most characteristic flight outline of all the birds of prey (see silhouette page) and is virtually an avian proto-type of the delta-winged aircraft. The white underwing has a narrow black trailing edge in the female, while the male has a broad black band that indents into the wing. When perched, it appears thick-set and tailless, and it is further identifiable by its black plumage which is relieved by a red back and tail, grey 'shoulders' and vivid red face and legs. Young birds are wholly brown when they leave the nest, but their characteristic shape, both perched and in flight, readily distinguishes them. It takes seven years to attain full adult plumage.

Distribution It occurs throughout the park.

Notes This species is usually seen flying rapidly across country rocking slightly from side to side as it adjusts to the air currents. It is probably from this that it was given its French name, one translation of which is 'tightrope walker'. The swaying flight is reminiscent of an acrobat with his long balanc-ing pole. The Bateleur feeds on a wide variety of mammals, birds and snakes as well as on carrion. It is capable of killing an adult guineafowl. It builds either a small stick nest of its own, or takes over the abandoned nest of some other large bird of prey. A single egg is laid about January.

23 COQUI FRANCOLIN (R.173)
Plate 7

Identification This is a small brown partridge-like bird. The male has an orange head and neck, but the female is rather more drab. A male is illus-trated.

Distribution It occurs in all areas and is quite common in the mixed scrub woodland on the main road between Main Camp and Shumba.

Notes It is almost always seen in pairs, usually when crossing a road. When thus encountered it moves very slowly and cautiously, keeping very low to the ground so that it appears to have no legs. If one drives up very slowly, it permits a close approach. Once it has crossed the road and moved into vegetation, it simply melts from sight. It has a characteristic call 'swem-pi, swem-pi' from which it obtains its popular name of 'Swempi'.

24 RED-BILLED FRANCOLIN (R.182)
Plate 7

Identification This brown francolin is readily identified by its red bill and legs, the yellow ring round its eye and its finely barred underparts.

Distribution It is confined to open areas on Kalahari sand and is common in the vicinity of Main Camp.

Notes It is often to be seen feeding out in the open beside roads, and it has the habit of scratching in elephant droppings in search of food. This is the francolin most likely to be found perched in a low tree or bush.

25 SWAINSON'S FRANCOLIN (R.185)
Plate 7

Identification This species is easy to recognize because of the bare red skin on the throat and round its eye. The body is dark brown and the bill and legs are black.

Distribution It occurs throughout the park, but not usually in thick woodland.

Notes Its harsh crowing call, especially at dawn and sunset, is one of the characteristic calls of the park. Its feeding habits are similar to those of the Red-billed Francolin.

26 CROWNED GUINEAFOWL (R.192)
Plate 7

Identification The spotted plumage, bare blue face and neck and the red casque on top of the head render this species unmistakable.

Distribution It is found in all areas.

Notes This is the most common gamebird in the park and it may gather at a drinking place in flocks of two hundred birds or more. Much of its time is spent feeding, but occasionally individuals will break off and indulge in a wild chase. During the rains the birds pair up for breeding. The nest is a scrape in the ground in a site well concealed by vegetation. About a dozen thick-shelled eggs are laid, but often clutches are much larger and these are probably the work of two females. The call is a monotonous double note repeated over and over from which various onomatopoeic African names for this species are derived.

27 CROWNED CRANE (R.214)
Plate 4

Identification This vivid species may be immediately identified by the straw coloured crown on top of its head. The call is a deep musical 'ma-hem'.

Distribution It occurs sparingly throughout the park, usually in association with pans or open marshy areas. The Main Camp area is a favourable locality in which to see it.

Notes This species feeds on aquatic life, insects and vegetable matter. In the park it is usually seen in pairs, but in farming areas it gathers in large flocks which may pose a serious problem to young grain crops. Breeding takes place during the rains, and pairs may be seen indulging in a graceful court-ship dance during which they bound round each other with spread wings. The nest is a pad of vegetation in a marshy area amongst tall grass or reeds. Two to four large white eggs are laid.

28 RED-CRESTED KORHAAN (R.224)
Plate 4

Identification   In shape this species resembles a miniature Ostrich. It is mainly brown in colour with a black belly. Females are drabber than males and lack grey on top of the head. A male is illustrated. The red crest is *not* a useful aid to identification as it is absent in the female and is only fluffed out by the male during display.

Distribution   It is confined mainly to areas of Kalahari sand and is quite common in the mixed scrub woodland between Main Camp and Shumba.

Notes   One usually sees this species as it cautiously crosses a road. The male is often heard making his crescendo whistling note from thick bush, and it is at the climax of this that he fluffs out his powder-puff red crest at the back of his head. He also rises to some height in a display flight before dropping like a stone as if shot; at the last minute he opens his wings and breaks his fall. No nest is made, the clutch of one or two eggs merely being laid on the bare ground.

29 THREE-BANDED SANDPLOVER (R.238)
Plate 8

Identification   This small plover is brown above and white below. The two black bands across the chest and the white area between them gives the 'three-banded' effect. It has a white eyebrow stripe, the bill is red at its base with a black tip and there is a red ring round the eye.

Distribution   It occurs in all areas where there is water.

Notes   This active species likes bare areas near water where it is usually seen running along the shore in search of insects. It makes a high-pitched 'peep, peep, peep' call and bobs its body while making it. No nest is constructed and the eggs are laid on the bare ground amongst stone chips or animal droppings. The eggs are covered with a mass of fine scrawls and are very difficult to see.

30 CROWNED PLOVER (R.242)
Plate 8

Identification   This species may be recognized by its brown upperparts and breast which contrast with the white abdomen. The top half of the head is black with a white ring on the crown from which the bird gets its name. The long legs are red and the bill is red with a black tip.

Distribution   It occurs in all areas where there are open expanses of short vegetation.

Notes   This is a common bird, particularly along the road between Main Camp and Shumba. During its extended breeding season, from about May to October, it may be found nesting in gravel chips on the road verges. The normal clutch is three eggs which are khaki in colour with black blotches and very difficult to see. The eggs are merely laid in a shallow scrape, as is the case with most plovers. Its Afrikaans name, 'Kiewietjie', describes its ringing call.

31 BLACKSMITH PLOVER (R.245)
Plate 8

Identification   The striking black and white plumage immediately identifies this plover. Its call, which gives it its name, is a distinctive metallic 'klink, klink, klink' like a hammer on an anvil.

Distribution   It is found throughout the park, but always in open areas and particularly at pans such as Nyamandhlovu, Guvalala and Ngweshla. It is plentiful at the Main Camp end of the park.

Notes   Like the Crowned Plover, it is often found beside roads. It has the habit of searching amongst elephant droppings for food. Its nest and eggs are similar to those of the Crowned Plover, but it is usually situated near water.

White-backed Vulture

Lappet-faced Vulture

PLATE 5

White-headed Vulture

Bateleur

Tawny Eagle

Fish Eagle

PLATE 6

Black-shouldered Kite

Yellow-billed Kite

Crowned Guineafowl

Coqui Francolin (male)

PLATE 7

Swainson's Francolin

Red-billed Francolin

Blacksmith Plover

Crowned Plover

PLATE 8

Wood Sandpiper

Three-banded Sandplover

Double-banded Sandgrouse
(male)

Namaqua Dove (male)

PLATE 9

Turtle Dove

Laughing Dove

Swallow-tailed Bee-eater

European Bee-eater

PLATE 10

Pied Kingfisher (male)

Carmine Bee-eater

Lilac-breasted Roller

Purple Roller

PLATE 11

Red-billed Hoopoe

Hoopoe

Grey Hornbill (male)

Bradfield's Hornbill

PLATE 12

Ground Hornbill

Red-billed Hornbill

32 WOOD SANDPIPER (R.264)
Plate 8

Identification This medium sized wader is dark brown above with white spots on its back and wings. The dull brown head, neck and breast merge into a white abdomen. There is a thin white stripe above the eye and the long bill is black. Its legs are dark olive green.

Distribution It is found in all localities, but always in association with water.

Notes This migrant from Europe and Asia is the most common wader in the park and is present from August until late April or early May. Some individuals may stay over for the winter. It is usually to be seen running actively along the shore or wading in shallow water as it searches for food.

33 DOUBLE-BANDED SANDGROUSE (R.310)
Plate 9

Identification The main colour of the male is brown with white spots on his wings and back. Across his chest he has two bands, one black and the other white, and his white forehead has a black band across it. His bill is orange and the bare skin round his large dark eye is yellow. The female lacks these distinctive features and is a drab mottled brown. A male is illustrated.

Distribution Although it may occur in all areas, it is most likely to be found west of Shumba, usually in association with mopane woodland.

Notes This partridge-like gamebird is usually seen as it crosses a road. Its short legs give it a very squat appearance not unlike the Coqui Francolin. During the breeding season from about July to October it is usually seen in pairs. At sundown it gathers in flocks and flies to the nearest waterhole to drink. Its attractive salmon-pink eggs are laid on the bare ground and the downy chicks leave the nest almost immediately. The parents carry water to their young by soaking their belly feathers which are specially adapted to retain moisture.

34 TURTLE DOVE (R.316)
Plate 9

Identification This large grey dove is readily identified by the black collar at the back of its neck. The call is a pleasant 'coo-coor' repeated over and over again.

Distribution Although found in all areas, it may be locally very common at times.

Notes Like all doves it is mainly a seed eater and therefore needs to drink regularly. When drinking, it does not lift its head between sips as do other birds. Instead it keeps its bill under water and sucks. The nest is a flimsy platform of sticks on which two white eggs are laid.

35 LAUGHING DOVE (R.317)
Plate 9

Identification It may be distinguished from the Turtle Dove by the pinkish wash to its plumage and by the fact that it lacks a collar. The breast is reddish speckled with black.

Distribution It occurs in all areas and is more likely to be found in the camps than is the Turtle Dove.

Notes The diet and nesting habits of this species are similar to those of the Turtle Dove. Its call, from which it gets its name, is a pleasant bubbling note that descends the scale.

36 NAMAQUA DOVE (R.318)
Plate 9

Identification This small dove has long pointed tail feathers that distinguish it from the other doves. The plumage is grey, the female being plain while the male has a mask and bib of black. His bill is orange while the female's is black. Both sexes show red in the wing in flight. A male is illustrated.

Distribution It is found in all areas, but it favours drier country.

Notes It is usually flushed from roads as one drives along and it flies away with a very rapid wing beat. The nest is always placed low down and the eggs are pale yellowish.

37 MEYER'S PARROT (R.327)
Plate 16

Identification It has a brown head and back with green underparts. The best guide to identification is the yellow shoulder patch which shows up well when the bird is perched and in flight. Adults have a yellow patch on the crown of the head, but this is absent in sub-adult birds. A sub-adult is illustrated.

Distribution It is found throughout the park where there is woodland, and it comes to the mulberry trees in Robins Camp when these are in fruit.

Notes One usually sees this species as it flies past very fast with rapid wing beats. In the foliage of a tree it is extraordinarily difficult to detect, and one's attention is usually attracted by its call. This is a series of piercing shrieks which sound as if someone has stuck a hot needle between the bird's shoulder blades! It feeds on fruit and berries and nests in a hole in a tree.

38 GREY LOERIE (R.339)
Plate 13

Identification This is a large grey bird with a longish tail and a crest.

Distribution It is found in all areas.

Notes One's attention is usually drawn by the call which is a loud scolding 'gweh', and it is from this that it gets its popular name of 'Go-away Bird'. The nest is a dove-like platform of sticks and the round eggs are the size of table tennis balls. Its food is mainly fruit and berries.

39 PIED KINGFISHER (R.394)
Plate 10

Identification The black and white plumage pattern makes this species unmistakable. A male is illustrated; females have a single band only across the chest.

Distribution It is found in all areas in association with water.

Notes This species is usually noticed as it hovers a few metres above the surface of the water watching for fish. When one is spotted, it drops head first into the water with a splash, and then emerges with a fish which it takes to a favourite perch where it is beaten to death. The nest is a tunnel of about one and a half metres excavated in a bank. At the end of it there is a chamber in which the round white eggs are laid.

40 EUROPEAN BEE-EATER (R.404)
Plate 10

Identification This attractive species is chestnut above and turquoise below with a yellow throat. The central tail feathers are elongated.

Distribution It occurs in all areas.

Notes This migrant from Europe and Asia is present in Rhodesia from about September to March. It is usually seen in flocks hawking insects on the wing, but it will also hunt from a perch. Its call is a pleasant liquid note that carries over a considerable distance.

41 CARMINE BEE-EATER (R.407)
Plate 10

Identification This exquisite species ranks as one of Africa's most beautiful birds. Its carmine colour immediately distinguishes it; and the top of its head and its rump are turquoise. The elongated tail feathers add another touch of grace to its appearance. Young birds are less colourful versions of the adult.

Distribution It is found in all areas but prefers open country.

Notes This species is present in Rhodesia from August to March and breeds while it is here. It winters further north in Africa, mainly in Tanzania. On the wing it is particularly graceful, but it also hunts from a perch and often sits on the ground. The nest is a tunnel in a bank, like that of a kingfisher. However, it breeds colonially, so that several hundred birds may breed side by side in a stretch of river bank. A breeding colony is one of the most spectacular sights in Africa.

42 SWALLOW-TAILED BEE-EATER (R.411)
Plate 10

Identification Although much smaller than the previous two species, this bee-eater is nevertheless attractive in its own right. It may be recognized by its green colour, yellow throat and forked tail.

Distribution It occurs in all areas.

Notes It hunts from a perch and is usually seen in twos or threes. The nest is a tunnel in the ground or low bank. A fairly similar species (not illustrated) that may be seen is the Little Bee-eater (R.410) which may be distinguished by its square tail and buff instead of green underparts.

43 LILAC-BREASTED ROLLER (R.413)
Plate 11

Identification The greenish-brown upperparts, lilac breast and turquoise abdomen render the perched bird attractive enough; but when it flies the blue and turquoise on its wings make it spectacular. It is often called a 'Blue Jay' because its colourful wings resemble those of the European Jay. The outer tail feathers are elongated.

Distribution   It occurs in all localities, except very thick woodland.

Notes   It hunts for insects from a perch, dropping down with a flash of colour to capture them. The name 'roller' is taken from the tumbling display flight performed during the breeding season to the accompaniment of harsh rasping notes. The nest is a natural hole in a tree.

44   PURPLE ROLLER   (R.415)
Plate 11

Identification   This roller is more 'chunky' in appearance than the previous species, lacks the elongated tail feathers and is comparatively less colourful. It is greenish above with a marked white eye stripe; below, it is pale mauve with heavy white streaking. On its shoulders and tail it is purple, but this does not show up well when it is perched.

Distribution   It occurs in all areas.

Notes   It is subject to local movement and leaves Rhodesia from about February to May. Like the Lilac-breasted Roller it hunts from a perch and feeds on insects. It also nests in a hole in a tree, and the illustration shows a bird leaving its nest.

45   HOOPOE   (R.418)
Plate 11

Identification   The crest, chestnut body and black and white wings make this species easy to identify.

Distribution   It is found in all areas.

Notes   It feeds on a variety of insects and their grubs, and walks rapidly about probing with its long bill as it goes. When alarmed or excited it raises its folded crest like a fan. The call is a mellow 'hoop, hoop' that is ventriloquial and carries over long distances. It usually nests in a hole in the ground or in a tree.

46 RED-BILLED HOOPOE (R.419)
Plate 11

Identification   This species may be recognized by its black plumage (iridescent dark green when the sun catches it), long tail and red bill and feet. In flight it reveals white spots on the tail and white patches in the wing.

Distribution   It is found in all areas of woodland.

Notes   This species spends its time clambering about trees probing for insects. It occurs in small groups of about four to six birds. One's attention is usually attracted by the extremely noisy chattering call as various members of the party keep in touch with each other. It nests in holes in trees and several birds help to feed the chicks.

47 GREY HORNBILL (R.424)
Plate 12

Identification   The drab grey colour and prominent white eyebrow stripe are the best guides to identification. The male has a small patch of yellow on the upper mandible as well as a slight casque; the female lacks this and her upper mandible is almost entirely yellow. A male is illustrated. The call is a whistling 'pew' that carries far.

Distribution   It occurs in most areas but is subject to seasonal movements.

Notes   It feeds on fruit and insects and tends to forage on the ground much less than the other hornbills. The nest is a natural cavity in a tree, the entrance being almost sealed with mud and droppings to form a narrow slit. The female remains imprisoned within and is fed by the male. During her time in the nest she moults and regrows all her tail and wing feathers. When the chicks are about a month old she breaks out, and the young seal up the entrance by themselves. Breeding commences in about October. Except in the case of the Ground Hornbill, the nesting habits of the other hornbills are similar.

48 RED-BILLED HORNBILL (R.425)
Plate 12

Identification Its *red* bill is rather thin and noticeably decurved compared with that of the other hornbills. The bill is adapted for digging and, in fact, this species spends much of its time feeding on the ground. Young birds have shorter bills which are dull red. The white on the head, dull red flesh on the bare throat and the white spots on the 'shoulders' of the wings also serve to identify it. The call is a high-pitched 'tock, tock, tock'.

Distribution It is a bird of mopane woodland and is thus found mainly from Shumba to Robins.

Notes Like the Yellow-billed Hornbill, it may become tame around picnic sites. In the dry season it forms large flocks. It feeds on insects, grubs and bulbs.

49 YELLOW-BILLED HORNBILL (R.426)
Front Cover

Identification The large *yellow* bill, white on the head and bold white spotting on the wings render this species easy to identify. Its 'tock, tock, tock' call, rather similar to that of the Red-billed Hornbill, is one of the most characteristic calls of the bushveld.

Distribution Although found throughout the park, it prefers open bush-veld rather than heavy woodland such as teak and mopane. It is most common at the Main Camp end of the park.

Notes It has become very tame around picnic sites and viewing platforms such as the one at Nyamandhlovu. In courtship, to an accompaniment of excited 'tock, tock, tock' calls, it raises spread wings above its back and hangs its head down. During this display the bare skin of its face and throat flushes red.

Grey Loerie

Fork-tailed Drongo

PLATE 13

Arrow-marked Babbler

Crested Barbet

Black-eyed Bulbul

Capped Wheatear

PLATE 14

Kurrichane Thrush

Groundscraper Thrush

Boubou Shrike

Long-tailed Shrike

PLATE 15

White-browed Sparrow-weaver

White-crowned Shrike

Meyer's Parrot

White Helmet Shrike

PLATE 16

Red-winged Starling (male)

Paradise Flycatcher (male)

50 BRADFIELD'S HORNBILL (R.428)
Plate 12

Identification This drab brown hornbill can only be confused with the Red-billed Hornbill. It differs in having an orange-red bill which is thicker and not as noticeably decurved, and a throat which is feathered and not bare. It is also brown on the head and breast and lacks the white spotting on the wings. The call is a mellow 'pip, pip, pip' quite different from that of the Red-billed Hornbill.

Distribution It occurs in Kalahari sandveld at the Main Camp end of the park, thus not overlapping the distribution of the Red-billed Hornbill.

Notes It forms flocks and wanders around in the dry season when it may be seen foraging on open ground near Main Camp.

51 GROUND HORNBILL (R.430)
Plate 12

Identification The large size (it is as big as a turkey), black plumage and bright red skin round the eye and on the throat render this species unmistakable. In flight it shows striking white wing tips. Immature birds lack red on on the face and throat. If a good view is obtained, females may be identified by a small patch of blue on the throat.

Distribution It may be seen throughout the park in a variety of habitats.

Notes This striking species occurs in small groups of about four to six birds which spend almost all their time walking in search of food. They fly reluctantly and usually alight after fifty metres or so. They have a deep booming call which carries over a great distance. The nest, a large cavity in a dead tree or a hollow amongst boulders, does not have a sealed entrance. Two white eggs are laid but, as far as is known, only one chick survives. The young bird joins the family group when it leaves the nest.

52 CRESTED BARBET (R.439)
Plate 13

Identification This colourful species has the strong bill characteristic of barbets. It may be readily identified by its orange-yellow head and under-parts and the black 'bib' across the breast. It is speckled black and white above, and there is a short crest at the back of the head. The call is a distinctive purring note like a two-stroke engine.

Distribution It is widely distributed in woodland and it is likely to be seen in camps and picnic sites.

Notes It feeds on insects and fruit and may spend much of its time on the ground. The nest is a hole excavated in a tree trunk in the manner of a woodpecker in which three to five white eggs are laid.

53 FORK-TAILED DRONGO (R.517)
Plate 13

Identification The black plumage and forked tail make this species easy to recognize.

Distribution It is common throughout the park in all habitats.

Notes This species perches conspicuously, usually low down, and watches for insects on which it feeds. It is an accomplished mimic and copies a wide variety of bird calls. The nest is a neat basin slung in the fork of a lateral branch. When breeding it is extremely aggressive, and it will relentlessly pursue hawks and eagles that have entered its territory.

54 ARROW-MARKED BABBLER (R.533)
Plate 13

Identification It is a dull brown bird with pointed flecks of white on its throat and breast. The eye is orange-red. It is best recognized by its habit of going round in chattering groups of about a dozen birds. The call is a raucous cacophany which becomes deafening when the birds are excited.

Distribution It is found in all localities, but prefers thick cover to open areas.

Notes This gregarious species forages for insects on the ground and the members of the party keep in touch with their chattering call. The nest is a deep cup placed in a creeper or thick shrubbery and the eggs are an attractive blue.

55 PIED BABBLER (R.536)
Plate 20

Identification This is a white bird that looks as if its tail and wings have been dipped in black ink. The bill is black and the eye is yellow. Like the Arrow-marked Babbler, it is characterized by its habit of going about in groups, but its call is not quite as raucous.

Distribution It is confined to Kalahari sand, usually where there are thorn trees. It should be watched for in Main Camp where it has become tame.

Notes The habits of this species are similar to those of the Arrow-marked Babbler. The blue eggs are unusual in that they are covered with small nodules. When the young leave the nest they are brownish, only moulting into white plummage later. However, as they remain in the family party, they should not be confused with the Arrow-marked Babbler.

56 BLACK-EYED BULBUL (R.545)
Plate 14

Identification The dull brown of its upperparts and chest merge to whitish on its abdomen. The best guides to identification are the yellow vent and the slightly crested black head. It has a cheerful call that has been rendered as 'come back to Calcutta'. A very similar species, the Red-eyed Bulbul, may be recognized by the red ring round its eye. It is rare in the park, although it has been seen in such varied localities as Ngweshla, Shumba and Big Toms.

Distribution　The Black-eyed Bulbul is common in all areas.

Notes　Although its diet is mainly fruit and insects, it has become tame in camps and picnic sites where it comes readily to search for scraps.

57　KURRICHANE THRUSH　(R.552)
Plate 14

Identification　The orange bill is the most distinctive feature of this thrush. Its upperparts are dull brown and it is orange below with a white throat and black 'moustache' streaks.

Distribution　It is found in all localities, but in woodland rather than open areas.

Notes　This species is likely to be seen in the camps as it forages on the ground for insects, and it has become very tame in places. The nest is a deep cup-shaped structure placed in the fork of a tree in which it lays blue spotted eggs.

58　GROUNDSCRAPER　THRUSH　(R.557)
Plate 14

Identification　This species may be recognized by its short tail, dull brown upperparts, boldly spotted white underparts and the two vertical black streaks near the eye. It has the habit of flicking its wings open and folding them again.

Distribution　It is found throughout the park in association with woodland.

Notes　Like the Kurrichane Thrush it feeds on insects on the ground. It has a very upright stance and, after running a short way, stops and flicks its wings. The nest is similar to that of the Kurrichane Thrush.

59 CAPPED WHEATEAR (R.568)
Plate 14

Identification   This species may be recognized by the broad black gorget that runs up the sides of its neck on to the face. There is a marked white eyebrow stripe, and the throat and abdomen are white. The legs appear very long for the size of the bird.

Distribution   It occurs in all areas where there are bare open spaces.

Notes   This dry season visitor to Rhodesia is present from May to November. It feeds on insects and prefers areas that are heavily overgrazed. A favourite perch is a termite mound or rock on which it stands with a typical upright posture. The nest is built in a hole underground, often inside a damaged termite's nest.

60 ARNOT'S CHAT (R.574)
Plate 20

Identification   The male is a black bird with a white shoulder patch and crown. The female has white shoulders and throat but is brown on top of the head. A male is illustrated.

Distribution   This species is characteristic of mopane woodland, although it may be found in other woodland at times. It is most likely to be seen west of Shumba.

Notes   One's attention is usually caught by its striking black and white pattern, especially as it may occur in thick woodland where there are few other birds to be seen. Much of its time is spent foraging for insects low down on the trunks of trees. Its nest is in a hollow in a tree.

61 PARADISE FLYCATCHER (R.682)
Plate 16

Identification   This exquisite species may be readily identified by its rich chestnut back and tail. The underparts and crested head are blue-grey. The male, which is illustrated, has two elongated central tail feathers.

Distribution   It is found in all areas in woodland.

Notes   This summer migrant to Rhodesia from further north in Africa is present from about October to March. It is an active species that spends much of its time hawking insects. The nest is a neat cup built on a pendant branch and camouflaged with lichens.

62   BOUBOU   (R.709)
Plate 15

Identification   This shrike is white below and black above with a white bar which runs down the length of the wing.

Distribution   It is found in all areas and is particularly common in Sinamatella Camp.

Notes   It prefers thick cover from which it descends to forage for insects on the ground. The call, although it sounds as if made by a single bird, is in fact a duet. There are two varieties, one a whistle answered by a rasping note, and the other a harsh 'kwe-oo' answered by a deep frog-like 'kwok-kwok'.

63   CRIMSON-BREASTED SHRIKE   (R.711)
Back cover

Identification   This striking species resembles the Boubou except that its underparts are crimson.

Distribution   It prefers dry thorn country and is therefore most likely to be seen on Kalahari sand at the Main Camp end of the park.

Notes   Its diet and habits are similar to those of the Boubou. The call is a duet which is even more integrated than that of the Boubou. The male makes a loud 'pew' followed by a rasping 'tjer-ru' from his mate and concluded with another 'pew' from the male. The whole call is made with such precision that it is hard to believe that two birds are involved. The nest is a cup made of bark strips and placed in the fork of a tree.

64 LONG-TAILED SHRIKE (R.724)
Plate 15

Identification The long black tail, black plumage and white on the wing make this species easy to identify. It reveals a white back in flight. The call is a harsh ratchet-like note but it also has a pleasant whistling song.

Distribution It is found in all areas in open country and is particularly common in and around Main Camp.

Notes This species perches conspicuously, usually on a dead tree from which it watches for insects. It quite often occurs in groups of several birds. The nest, an untidy collection of dry grass with a neat cup in the centre, is placed in a thorn tree.

65 WHITE HELMET SHRIKE (R.727)
Plate 16

Identification This shrike is characteristically marked, both when perched and in flight. The back, wings and tail are black. The wings have a bar of white running down their length and the outer tail feathers are white. The neck and underparts are white and the face is grey. The most distinctive feature, if a good view is obtained, is the yellow eye surrounded by a bare yellow ring which makes the eye seem very large.

Distribution Although found in all areas, it is a bird of woodland and not open country.

Notes It is a gregarious species that may be seen in parties of up to about twelve birds. It searches for insects low down on tree trunks or on the ground. The nest is a neat cup bound externally with cobwebs. Several birds assist in feeding the chicks.

66 WHITE-CROWNED SHRIKE (R.730)
Plate 15

Identification It may be recognized by the white crown, breast and throat which contrast with the dark brown on its face and neck. The upperparts and tail are also brown. It gives the impression of having a very large head. In flight its wing beats are rapid and dove-like.

Distribution It occurs in all localities but is not found in very thick woodland. The open country round Main Camp is a good area in which to see it.

Notes It usually occurs in pairs or small groups and hunts for insects from a perch. Although larger, the nest is similar to that of the White Helmet Shrike. Several birds help to feed the young.

67 PLUM-COLOURED STARLING (R.736)
Plate 17

Identification The males are readily identifiable by the white underparts which are neatly divided from their iridescent plum-coloured breasts and backs. In some lights their plumage glows like hot coals. The females and young birds are drab brown above and have white underparts which are heavily streaked with black. In plate 17 males and females are shown together at a bird bath.

Distribution It is found in all areas.

Notes This species comes from further north in Africa and only occurs in Rhodesia from about September to May. It gathers in large flocks, except when breeding which takes place from late October to about December. The nest is a hole in a tree which is lined with green leaves.

Plum-coloured Starling

Yellow-billed Oxpecker

PLATE 17

Blue-eared Glossy Starling

Long-tailed Glossy Starling

House Sparrow (female)

Masked Weaver (male)

PLATE 18

House Sparrow (male)

Grey-headed Sparrow

Red-headed Weaver (male)

Scarlet-chested Sunbird (male)

PLATE 19

Golden-breasted Bunting

Blue Waxbill

Pied Babbler

PLATE 20

Arnot's Chat (male)

Yellow-eye Canary

68 BLUE-EARED GLOSSY STARLING (R.738)
Plate 17

Identification This species may be easily identified by its glossy blue-green plumage and orange eye.

Distribution It is found most often at the Main Camp end of the park and is common in Main Camp itself.

Notes This attractive bird has become very tame and usually comes along when people arrive at the viewing platforms at Nyamandhlovu and Guva-lala. It eats both insects and fruit, but it is also partial to scraps. The nest site is a hole in a tree or metal fence post, and it always adds a sloughed snake skin to its nest lining of feathers.

69 LONG-TAILED GLOSSY STARLING (R.742)
Plate 17

Identification This starling may be identified by its glossy blue-green plumage, long tail, long legs and *black* eye. The call is a harsh 'skwee-ya'.

Distribution It is found almost entirely west of Shumba, particularly in association with mopane woodland.

Notes If the visitor is travelling west from Main Camp on the main tar road, his first sighting of this starling will probably be at Shumba picnic site. After this point, whether he travels to Robins or Sinamatella, he will find that it is everywhere common. Its habits are similar to those of the Blue-eared Glossy Starling.

70 RED-WINGED STARLING (R.745)
Plate 16

Identification This large *black* starling is easily recognized by its red wing tips. The female is grey on the head and in both sexes the eye is black. A male is illustrated. The call is a pleasant whistling 'pee-ju'.

Distribution Although normally a bird of rocky country where there are cliffs, this species may be encountered in several places in the park. There is a tame pair resident at Shumba, but these starlings also occur at Robins and Sinamatella.

Notes It feeds on insects, fruit and scraps. The nest is normally placed on a cliff, but it has adapted to breeding in buildings as well.

71 YELLOW-BILLED OXPECKER (R.747)
Plate 17

Identification It may be recognized by its brown colour, red eye and yellow bill which has a red tip. The pale back shows up well in flight. Young birds have dark bills. Another very similar species is the Red-billed Oxpecker, which may be distinguished by its red bill and the fact that it does not have a pale back in flight.

Distribution It is found in all areas.

Notes This gregarious species is always found in association with big game animals. Its sharp claws and stiff tail feathers are adaptations for clambering over animals in search of ticks which are its main food. At the approach of danger it will warn its host by flying about and making a chattering call. The nest is a thick pad of hair placed in a hole in a tree.

72 SCARLET-CHESTED SUNBIRD (R.774)
Plate 19

Identification The small size, black plumage, red chest and long curved bill make the male easy to identify. In certain lights the iridescent green patches on his throat and on top of his head show up well. The female is a dull brown bird and she is not readily distinguished from the females of other sunbirds. The call is a lively 'tjip, tjip, tjip, tjip'. A male is illustrated. During the rains a sunbird of similar size, the Black Sunbird (R.773), is common in the teak trees of Main Camp. The plumage of the male of this species, which is not illustrated, is entirely black.

Distribution It is found in all areas.

Notes The long bill is adapted for probing flowers for nectar and, like all sunbirds, it is particularly attracted to aloes. It also feeds on insects, particularly when feeding its young. The nest is an oval of dry plant material warmly lined with feathers and suspended at the end of a branch.

73 WHITE-BROWED SPARROW-WEAVER (R.780)
Plate 15

Identification It is brown above and dull whitish below. The most distinguishing feature is the white eyebrow stripe.

Distribution This bird is very widely distributed and it occurs in all habitats.

Notes This cheerful species is probably one of the most characteristic birds in the park and it occurs in all the camps and at most of the picnic sites where it has become very tame. It feeds on insects, seeds and scraps. The nest is an untidy dome of straw with the entrance underneath and, as they breed colonially, there are a number of nests in the same tree. This bird is a fine songster, and one usually awakes to its musical calls which build up into a crescendo of liquid notes.

74 HOUSE SPARROW (R.784)
Plate 18

Identification The male may be identified by the black patch on his throat. He is reddish above and white below. Except for her white eyebrow, the female has no characteristic markings and is drab light brown. The call is a lively chirping.

Distribution   It occurs in Main Camp and Robins, but it had not apparently reached Sinamatella by 1973.

Notes   This species was introduced into South Africa at East London and Durban at about the turn of the century. After a sedentary existence up to the 1950s, it suddenly 'exploded' in spectacular fashion and colonized most of southern Africa. First arrivals in Rhodesia were probably in about 1956, and during the following decade the whole country was colonized. It had not apparently reached Wankie National Park by 1963. It is a lively species that always occurs in association with man. Its diet consists of seeds, insects and scraps. The nest is an untidy ball of straw placed under the roof of a building.

75   GREY-HEADED SPARROW   (R.787)
Plate 18

Identification   Unlike the House Sparrow, the sexes are similar in this species. It is mainly grey and therefore the grey head does not show up well. A useful guide to identification is the plain reddish shoulder which has a white bar. The rump is also reddish. The call is a chattering note.

Distribution   It is found in all areas.

Notes   Although found in the camps, this species is not dependant on man like the House Sparrow. Its habits are similar except that it usually nests in a hole in a tree.

76   RED-HEADED WEAVER   (R.793)
Plate 19

Identification   The red head, bill, chest and upper back make the male unmistakable. The female is dull yellowish with no red colouration at all. A male is illustrated.

Distribution   It occurs in all areas and breeds in all three camps.

Notes This species breeds during the early summer months; during the winter the male loses his red plumage and resembles the female. The nest is a characteristic retort-shaped structure woven by the male from thin bark strips. Nests are particularly common in Robins camp and are even attached to buildings instead of pendant branches.

77 MASKED WEAVER (R.803)
Plate 18

Identification With his red eye, black mask and yellow body, a breeding male is unmistakable. Females have no mask and are dull yellowish. During the winter months the male loses his black mask.

Distribution It occurs in all areas, but the best place to see it is in Main Camp.

Notes This species is usually noticed during its extended summer breeding season when the males are building their kidney-shaped nests. To attract a female they hang upside down beneath the nest and flap their wings to the accompaniment of an excited swizzling call (see silhouettes).

78 BLUE WAXBILL (R.839)
Plate 19

Identification This diminutive species may be readily identified by its grey upperparts and attractive blue underparts. The call is a lively succession of 'tseet, tseet, tseet' notes.

Distribution It is found in all areas.

Notes This species is a common visitor to bird baths in the camps and picnic sites. Its diet is seeds and insects such as termites. The nest is an untidy ball of grass and it is frequently situated near a wasp's nest.

79 YELLOW-EYE CANARY (R.859)
Plate 20

Identification This attractive species may be identified by its yellow underparts, grey head and the prominent yellow eyebrow. In flight it reveals a yellow rump.

Distribution It is found in all areas.

Notes Like the Blue Waxbill, it is usually seen when it comes to drink, quite often in small flocks. The nest is a neat cup warmly lined with downy material and placed in a fork in a tree. It breeds towards the end of the rainy season when seeds are most plentiful.

80 GOLDEN-BREASTED BUNTING (R.874)
Plate 19

Identification This is a colourful species which may be recognized by its rich orange-yellow underparts, red back and black face with white streaks above and below the eye.

Distribution It occurs in all areas in woodland.

Notes Like all seed eaters it needs to drink regularly and is most likely to be seen at water. The nest is a grass cup placed in a bush or small tree. The white eggs have black scrawls on them, hence the schoolboy nickname 'Scribbler'.

A check list of birds recorded in Wankie National Park

(The names and numbers follow *Roberts Birds of South Africa* 1970.)

1	Ostrich	80	White Stork
6	Dabchick	81	Sacred Ibis
41	Pink-backed Pelican	83	Glossy Ibis
42	White Pelican	85	African Spoonbill
50	Reed Cormorant	86	Greater Flamingo
52	Darter	87	Lesser Flamingo
54	Grey Heron	88	Spurwing Goose
55	Black-headed Heron	89	Egyptian Goose
56	Goliath Heron	91	Knob-billed Duck
57	Purple Heron	92	Pygmy Goose
58	Great White Egret	94	Cape Shoveler
59	Little Egret	95	Black Duck
60	Yellow-billed Egret	97	Red-billed Teal
61	Cattle Egret	98	Cape Teal
62	Squacco Heron	99	Hottentot Teal
63	Green-backed Heron	100	White-faced Whistling Duck
64	Black Heron	101	Fulvous Whistling Duck
66	Dwarf Bittern	102	Red-eyed Pochard
67	Little Bittern	103	Maccoa Duck
69	Night Heron	104	White-backed Duck
70	White-backed Night Heron	105	Secretary Bird
72	Hamerkop	106	Cape Vulture
73	Marabou	107	White-backed Vulture
74	Openbill	108	Lappet-faced Vulture
75	Saddlebill	109	White-headed Vulture
76	Wood Stork	110	Hooded Vulture
77	Woolly-necked Stork	113	Peregrine
78	White-bellied Stork	114	Lanner
79	Black Stork	115	Hobby

116	African Hobby	166	European Marsh Harrier
117	Red-necked Falcon	168	Pallid Harrier
119	Eastern Red-footed Kestrel	170	Montagu's Harrier
120	Western Red-footed Kestrel	171	Gymnogene
121	Dickinson's Kestrel	172	Osprey
122	Greater Kestrel	173	Coqui Francolin
123	Rock Kestrel	174	Crested Francolin
125	Lesser Kestrel	177	Shelley's Francolin
127	Cuckoo Falcon	182	Red-billed Francolin
128	Black Kite	183	Natal Francolin
129	Yellow-billed Kite	185	Swainson's Francolin
130	Black-shouldered Kite	190	Harlequin Quail
131	Bat Hawk	192	Crowned Guineafowl
133	Black Eagle	193	Crested Guineafowl
134	Tawny Eagle	196	Kurrichane Button Quail
135	Steppe Eagle	198	Corncrake
136	Lesser Spotted Eagle	199	African Crake
137	Wahlberg's Eagle	202	Baillon's Crake
139	Booted Eagle	203	Black Crake
140	Ayres' Hawk Eagle	208	Purple Gallinule
141	African Hawk Eagle	209	Lesser Gallinule
142	Martial Eagle	210	Moorhen
144	Lizard Buzzard	211	Lesser Moorhen
145	Brown Snake Eagle	212	Red-knobbed Coot
146	Black-breasted Snake Eagle	213	Peter's Finfoot
149	Fish Eagle	214	Crowned Crane
151	Bateleur	215	Wattled Crane
153	Augur Buzzard	217	Kori Bustard
154	Steppe Buzzard	219	Stanley (Denham's) Bustard
157	Ovambo Sparrowhawk	224	Red-crested Korhaan
158	Little Sparrowhawk	227	Black-bellied Korhaan
159	Black Sparrowhawk	228	African Jacana
160	African Goshawk	229	Lesser Jacana
161	Little Banded Goshawk	230	Painted Snipe
162	Gabar Goshawk	235	White-fronted Sandplover
163	Dark Chanting Goshawk	237	Kittlitz's Sandplover
165	Chanting Goshawk	238	Three-banded Sandplover

240 Caspian Plover
242 Crowned Plover
244 Lesser Black-winged Plover
245 Blacksmith Plover
247 Wattled Plover
249 Great Snipe
253 Little Stint
256 Ruff
258 Common Sandpiper
259 Green Sandpiper
262 Marsh Sandpiper
263 Greenshank
264 Wood Sandpiper
269 Avocet
270 Stilt
274 Water Dikkop
275 Cape Dikkop
277 Temminck's Courser
279 Three-banded Courser
280 Bronze-wing Courser
282 Black-winged Pratincole
283 White-collared Pratincole
288 Grey-headed Gull
304 White-winged Black Tern
305 Whiskered Tern
306 Skimmer
308 Spotted Sandgrouse
309 Yellow-throated Sandgrouse
310 Double-banded Sandgrouse
314 Red-eyed Turtle Dove
316 Turtle Dove
317 Laughing Dove
318 Namaqua Dove
321 Emerald-spotted Wood Dove
323 Green Pigeon
326 Brown-necked Parrot
327 Meyer's Parrot

337 Purple-crested Loerie
339 Grey Loerie
340 European Cuckoo
341 African Cuckoo
343 Red-chested Cuckoo
344 Black Cuckoo
346 Great Spotted Cuckoo
347 Striped Cuckoo
348 Jacobin Cuckoo
351 Klaas's Cuckoo
352 Diederik Cuckoo
353 Black Coucal
355 Senegal Coucal
359 Barn Owl
361 Marsh Owl
363 Scops Owl
364 White-faced Owl
365 Pearl-spotted Owl
366 Barred Owl
368 Spotted Eagle Owl
369 Giant Eagle Owl
371 European Nightjar
372 Rufous-cheeked Nightjar
373 Fiery-necked Nightjar
374 Freckled Nightjar
376 Mozambique Nightjar
377 Pennant-wing Nightjar
378 European Swift
383 White-rumped Swift
384 Horus Swift
385 Little Swift
387 Palm Swift
392 Red-faced Mousebird
393 Narina Trogon
394 Pied Kingfisher
395 Giant Kingfisher
396 Half-collared Kingfisher

397	Malachite Kingfisher	456	Singing Bush Lark
398	Natal Kingfisher	458	Rufous-naped Lark
399	Woodland Kingfisher	459	Fawn-coloured Lark
401	Grey-hooded Kingfisher	460	Sabota Lark
402	Brown-hooded Kingfisher	464	Dusky Lark
403	Striped Kingfisher	468	Flappet Lark
404	European Bee-eater	484	Chestnut-backed Finch Lark
407	Carmine Bee-eater	485	Grey-backed Finch Lark
409	White-fronted Bee-eater	488	Red-capped Lark
410	Little Bee-eater	493	European Swallow
411	Swallow-tailed Bee-eater	495	White-throated Swallow
412	European Roller	496	Wire-tailed Swallow
413	Lilac-breasted Roller	498	Pearl-breasted Swallow
414	Racquet-tailed Roller	499	Grey-rumped Swallow
415	Purple Roller	500	Mosque Swallow
416	Broad-billed Roller	501	Red-breasted Swallow
418	Hoopoe	502	Greater Striped Swallow
419	Red-billed Hoopoe	503	Lesser Striped Swallow
421	Scimitar-billed Hoopoe	507	House Martin
422	Trumpeter Hornbill	508	European Sand Martin
424	Grey Hornbill	509	African Sand Martin
425	Red-billed Hornbill	510	Banded Sand Martin
426	Yellow-billed Hornbill	513	Black Cuckoo Shrike
427	Crowned Hornbill	515	White-breasted Cuckoo Shrike
428	Bradfield's Hornbill	517	Fork-tailed Drongo
430	Ground Hornbill	519	European Golden Oriole
431	Black-collared Barbet	520	African Golden Oriole
432	Pied Barbet	521	Black-headed Oriole
437	Yellow-fronted Tinker Barbet	522	Pied Crow
439	Crested Barbet	525	Grey Tit
440	Greater Honeyguide	527	Southern Black Tit
442	Lesser Honeyguide	530	Grey Penduline Tit
443	Sharp-billed Honeyguide	531	Cape Penduline Tit
446	Bennett's Woodpecker	533	Arrow-marked Babbler
447	Golden-tailed Woodpecker	536	Pied Babbler
450	Cardinal Woodpecker	544	Red-eyed Bulbul
451	Bearded Woodpecker	545	Black-eyed Bulbul

546	Terrestrial Bulbul		654	Spotted Flycatcher
550	Yellow-bellied Bulbul		656	Blue-grey Flycatcher
552	Kurrichane Thrush		657	Grey Tit-babbler
557	Groundscraper Thrush		668	Tit-babbler
562	Angola Thrush		661	Marico Flycatcher
568	Capped Wheatear		662	Mouse-coloured Flycatcher
570	Familiar Chat		664	Black Flycatcher
574	Arnot's Chat		673	Chin Spot Batis
575	Ant-eating Chat		682	Paradise Flycatcher
576	Stone Chat		685	African Pied Wagtail
580	Heuglin's Robin		689	Yellow Wagtail
585	Bearded Robin		692	Richard's Pipit
586	Kalahari Scrub Robin		695	Buffy Pipit
588	White-browed Scrub Robin		698	Tree Pipit
594	Whitethroat		702	Golden Pipit
596	Icterine Warbler		705	Pink-throated Longclaw
599	Willow Warbler		706	Lesser Grey Shrike
600	Yellow-bellied Eremomela		707	Fiscal Shrike
601	Burnt-necked Eremomela		708	Red-backed Shrike
602	Greencap Eremomela		709	Boubou
603	European Great Reed Warbler		711	Crimson-breasted Shrike
607	European Marsh Warbler		712	Puff back Shrike
608	European Sedge Warbler		714	Three-streaked Tchagra
614	Barred Warbler		715	Black-crowned Tchagra
621	Crombec		719	Orange-breasted Bush Shrike
622	Bar-throated Apalis		723	Grey-headed Bush Shrike
625	Yellow-breasted Apalis		724	Long-tailed Shrike
628	Grey-backed Bush Warbler		727	White Helmet Shrike
629	Fantail Cisticola		728	Red-billed Helmet Shrike
630	Desert Cisticola		730	White-crowned Shrike
637	Neddicky		731	Brubru Shrike
642	Rattling Cisticola		735	Wattled Starling
644	Red-faced Cisticola		736	Plum-coloured Starling
646	Le Vaillant's Cisticola		737	Cape Glossy Starling
647	Croaking Cisticola		738	Blue-eared Glossy Starling
649	Tawny-flanked Prinia		742	Long-tailed Glossy Starling
650	Black-chested Prinia		745	Red-winged Starling

747	Yellow-billed Oxpecker	823	Bronze Mannikin
748	Red-billed Oxpecker	829	Golden-backed Pytilia
754	Coppery Sunbird	830	Melba Finch
755	Marico Sunbird	835	Jameson's Firefinch
763	White-bellied Sunbird	837	Red-billed Firefinch
772	Black Sunbird	839	Blue Waxbill
774	Scarlet-chested Sunbird	840	Violet-eared Waxbill
777	Yellow White-eye	841	Black-cheeked Waxbill
779	Buffalo Weaver	843	Common Waxbill
780	White-browed Sparrow-weaver	844	Quail Finch
		846	Pin-tailed Whydah
784	House Sparrow	847	Shaft-tailed Whydah
787	Grey-headed Sparrow	849	Black Widow-finch
788	Yellow-throated Sparrow	851	Steel-blue Widow-finch
789	Scaly-feathered Finch	852	Paradise Whydah
793	Red-headed Weaver	853	Broad-tailed Paradise Whydah
797	Spotted-backed Weaver	854	Cuckoo Finch
803	Masked Weaver	859	Yellow-eye Canary
805	Red-billed Quelea	860	Black-throated Canary
808	Red Bishop	867	Streaky-headed Seed-eater
810	Cape Widow	868	Black-eared Seed-eater
812	Golden Bishop	871	Lark-like Bunting
814	White-winged Widow	872	Rock Bunting
821	Cut-throat Finch	874	Golden-breasted Bunting

Total as at 31st January 1974: 401 species

Route list

Route and date

1 Ostrich								
2 Grey Heron								
3 Great White Egret								
4 Cattle Egret								
5 Hamerkop								
6 Marabou								
7 Saddlebill								
8 Woolly-necked Stork								
9 White-bellied Stork								
10 White Stork								
11 Egyptian Goose								
12 Knob-billed Duck								
13 Red-billed Teal								
14 Secretary Bird								
15 White-backed Vulture								
16 Lappet-faced Vulture								
17 White-headed Vulture								
18 Yellow-billed Kite								
19 Black-shouldered Kite								
20 Tawny Eagle								
21 Fish Eagle								
22 Bateleur								
23 Coqui Francolin								

Route and date

24 Red-billed Francolin								
25 Swainson's Francolin								
26 Crowned Guineafowl								
27 Crowned Crane								
28 Red-crested Korhaan								
29 Three-banded Sandplover								
30 Crowned Plover								
31 Blacksmith Plover								
32 Wood Sandpiper								
33 Double-banded Sandgrouse								
34 Turtle Dove								
35 Laughing Dove								
36 Namaqua Dove								
37 Meyer's Parrot								
38 Grey Loerie								
39 Pied Kingfisher								
40 European Bee-eater								
41 Carmine Bee-eater								
42 Swallow-tailed Bee-eater								
43 Lilac-breasted Roller								
44 Purple Roller								
45 Hoopoe								
46 Red-billed Hoopoe								
47 Grey Hornbill								
48 Red-billed Hornbill								
49 Yellow-billed Hornbill								
50 Bradfield's Hornbill								
51 Ground Hornbill								
52 Crested Barbet								
53 Fork-tailed Drongo								
54 Arrow-marked Babbler								

Route and date

55 Pied Babbler						
56 Black-eyed Bulbul						
57 Kurrichane Thrush						
58 Groundscraper Thrush						
59 Capped Wheatear						
60 Arnot's Chat						
61 Paradise Flycatcher						
62 Boubou						
63 Crimson-breasted Shrike						
64 Long-tailed Shrike						
65 White Helmet Shrike						
66 White-crowned Shrike						
67 Plum-coloured Starling						
68 Blue-eared Glossy Starling						
69 Long-tailed Glossy Starling						
70 Red-winged Starling						
71 Yellow-billed Oxpecker						
72 Scarlet-chested Sunbird						
73 White-browed Sparrow-weaver						
74 House Sparrow						
75 Grey-headed Sparrow						
76 Red-headed Weaver						
77 Masked Weaver						
78 Blue Waxbill						
79 Yellow-eye Canary						
80 Golden-breasted Bunting						